HAMSTER PALS

Crabtree Publishing Company
www.crabtreebooks.com
1-800-387-7650

Published in Canada
Crabtree Publishing
616 Welland Avenue
St. Catharines, ON
L2M 5V6

Published in the United States
Crabtree Publishing
PMB 59051
350 Fifth Ave, 59th Floor
New York, NY 10118

Published in 2018 by CRABTREE PUBLISHING COMPANY.

First published in 2017 by Wayland
Copyright © Hodder and Stoughton, 2017

Author: Pat Jacobs

Editor: Elizabeth Brent

Project coordinator: Kathy Middleton

Editor: Petrice Custance

Cover and Interior Design: Dynamo

Proofreader: Wendy Scavuzzo

Prepress technician: Samara Parent

Print and production coordinator: Margaret Amy Salter

Photographs:
iStock: p1 lepas2004; p2 blacktomb, Lusyaya, Martina_L; p4 Shawn Ang; p6 Elena_Danileiko, Viachaslau Kraskouski; p7 Enskanto, Emilia Stasiak, ChrisPethick; p8 spectrelabs, Ilona Baha; p9 vladimirzahariev; p10 Tempusfugit; p11 Just_One_Pic; p12 Feng Yu, zevei-wenhui; p13 Cindernatalie, ultrapro; p14 eve_eve01genesis; p15 Eric Isselée, UroshPetrovic, chengyuzheng; p16 Pryshchepa Serii, anatols; p17 Kvkirillov; p19 Shawn Ang, Kingarion; p3, 20 Wolfhound911; p21 pisit38, Leonid Yastremskiy; p22 Eric Isselée, Alexandr Pakhnyushchyy, Felix_Adi; p23 Lusyaya; p24 vladimirzahariev; p25 fantom_rd, Anna Subbotina-Kononchuk; p27 vladimirzahariev; p28 AlexKalashnikov, Bedolaga; p29 IgorKovalchuk; p32 Felix_Adi; Front cover: Alona Rjabceva; Back cover: IgorKovalchuk

Shutterstock: p6 Subbotina Anna, DaCek; p7 Allocricetulus; p9 kowit1982; p10 Beth Van Trees; p13 Punyaphat Larpsomboon; p14 Piotr Wawrzyniuk; p24 Bildagentur Zoonar GmbH; p26 stock_shot; p27 LeonP, Robynrg;

Alamy: p5 Juniors Bildarchiv GmbH; p17 Maximilian Weinzierl; p18 Juniors Bildarchiv GmbH; p23 Nathan Hornby, Maximilian Weinzierl; p26 Aurum

Printed in the USA/072017/CG20170524

Library and Archives Canada Cataloguing in Publication

Jacobs, Pat, author
  Hamster pals / Pat Jacobs.

(Pet pals)
Includes index.
Issued in print and electronic formats.
ISBN 978-0-7787-3560-1 (hardcover).--
ISBN 978-0-7787-3582-3 (softcover).--
ISBN 978-1-4271-1947-6 (HTML)

    1. Hamsters as pets--Juvenile literature. 2. Hamsters--
Behavior--Juvenile literature. I. Title.

SF459.H3J34 2017   j636.935'6   C2017-902521-X
                                              C2017-902522-8

Library of Congress Cataloging-in-Publication Data

Names: Jacobs, Pat, author.
Title: Hamster pals / Pat Jacobs.
Description: New York, New York : Crabtree Publishing, 2018. |
    Series: Pet pals | Audience: Age 7-10. | Audience: Grade K to 3.
    | Includes index.
Identifiers: LCCN 2017016738 (print) | LCCN 2017027435 (ebook)
    ISBN 9781427119476 (Electronic HTML) |
    ISBN 9780778735601 (reinforced library binding) |
    ISBN 9780778735823 (pbk.)
Subjects: LCSH: Hamsters as pets--Juvenile literature.
Classification: LCC SF459.H3 (ebook) | LCC SF459.H3 J34 2018
    (print) | DDC 636.935/6--dc23
LC record available at https://lccn.loc.gov/2017016738

CONTENTS

YOUR HAMSTER
FROM HEAD TO TAIL

Every hamster has a different personality, but one thing all hamsters have in common is that they sleep during the day and are active in the evenings. In the wild, this behavior helps to protect them from **predators**.

Feet: Hamsters use their front feet to hold food and dig. Their back feet are larger to help them balance when they stand up.

Ears: Hamsters have very good hearing. They can hear **ultrasonic** sounds and use these to communicate without being heard by predators.

Eyes: Hamsters see better in dim light than in bright daylight. They are thought to be **color-blind**.

Nose: An excellent sense of smell helps hamsters find food, and also to recognize other hamsters and their owner.

Whiskers: Whiskers on a hamster's face and body help it to find its way around in the dark.

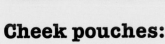

Teeth: Hamsters have large front teeth that grow throughout their lives, so they need to gnaw to stop them from growing too long.

Cheek pouches: Hamsters use their pouches to carry food to their **burrow**. The skin inside is dry and rough.

HAMSTER FACTS

- A Syrian hamster can carry up to half its own body weight in food in its cheek pouches, making its head up to three times its normal size.

- A hamster may travel up to 6 miles (10 km) a night on its exercise wheel.

HAMSTER BREEDS

There are four main **breeds** of pet hamsters: Syrian, Russian Dwarf, Roborovski, and Chinese. Syrian hamsters are loners, so you can only keep one to a cage, but Russian Dwarfs are usually happiest living with their pals.

Short-haired Syrian hamsters are sometimes called golden hamsters, but they can be found in up to 40 different colors.

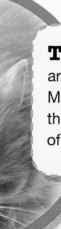

Teddy bear hamsters are long-haired Syrians. Males have a **ruff** around their neck and a long skirt of hair along their back.

Panda bear Syrian hamsters are black and white, as you might guess. White hamsters with black spots are known as Dalmatian hamsters.

Black bear hamsters are Syrians with all-black fur (all-white hamsters are called Polar Bears).

Campbell's Russian Dwarf hamsters have a dark stripe along their spine. They can live in single sex pairs or groups, as long as they have grown up together.

Roborovski hamsters are the smallest breed, but also the fastest, so they are difficult to handle. They should be kept in single-sex pairs or small groups.

Winter White Russian Dwarf (or Siberian) hamsters are similar to Campbell's Russian Dwarfs, but they don't have a dark stripe and they turn a lighter color in winter.

Chinese hamsters are a dwarf breed, with a slim body, a dark stripe along their spine, and a long tail. They are sometimes called "mousters" because they look like mice.

AVERAGE LIFESPAN

Syrian and Roborovski hamsters live for about three years, while Russian and Chinese breeds live for about two. It's best to buy or adopt hamsters that are four to six weeks old.

CHOOSING YOUR HAMSTER

Hamsters can begin making babies at a very young age, so males and females should be separated if they are more than five weeks old.

Syrian hamsters are twice the size of dwarf and Chinese hamsters, and they are easier to handle. If you're looking for a pet you can pick up and stroke, a Syrian hamster is the best choice.

SYRIAN HAMSTERS

Although Syrian hamsters live together happily as babies, as they grow older they will fight, and one may even kill the other. They are easier to **tame** than dwarf hamsters, and usually become good friends with their owner.

LONG-HAIRED HAMSTERS

Long-haired hamsters need regular grooming, especially the males. Bedding and food gets caught in their fur, so they should be brushed with a toothbrush at least once a week.

DWARF HAMSTERS

These cute little pets are usually happy living together, although males may sometimes fight. They are very fast and active animals, and most don't like being handled, but it's great fun watching them race around and play together.

CHINESE HAMSTERS

Although they are good-natured and rarely bite, Chinese hamsters are not often kept as pets because they are timid and very fast-moving. This makes them difficult to handle—and to catch if they escape. They can be **territorial** and may fight.

CHOOSING A PET

Hamsters are usually asleep during the day, but it's important to see them moving about to check that they don't have any health problems. If you can, it's best to visit the pet store in the evening, when hamsters are most likely to be active.

PET CHECK

- Hamsters should be lively and curious.
- Their coat should be clean and fluffy, with no wet or bare patches.
- Their breathing should be almost silent.
- Their front teeth should line up properly.

HAMSTER HOMES

Hamsters need an escape-proof cage that is easy to clean and has plenty of space to run and play. It's best to get the cage set up before bringing your new pet home, so it can start to settle in right away.

A solid wheel is safer than one with gaps because hamsters can get their legs stuck.

BORN TO RUN

A wheel provides plenty of exercise, but make sure it's large enough so your fully-grown hamster won't have to arch its back too much.

Cages should have solid floors because wire floors can damage hamsters' feet and legs.

I don't like to live near a TV, computer, vacuum cleaner, or running water because they make ultrasonic noises that disturb me.

There should be a sleeping area with space to build a nest, move around, and store food.

Cage bars should be a maximum of 1/4 inch (0.5 cm) apart for dwarf breeds. Tubes and ladders are often too steep for these tiny pets.

BEST BEDDING AND NESTING MATERIALS

- Recycled paper bedding or wood shavings make the best floor covering for hamsters. Sawdust, hay, and straw are too dusty for their delicate noses.

- White paper towels or toilet paper make perfect nesting materials. They won't cause problems if your hamster eats them or gets its legs caught in them.

The base should be deep enough for hamsters to dig through their bedding without scattering it everywhere.

HAPPY HAMMIES

Moving to a new home is stressful for a hamster. It will need a few days to get used to all the unfamiliar sounds and smells. Don't try to pick your pet up during this time, and never disturb it while it's sleeping.

HANDLING YOUR PET

When your hamster is happy to take food from you, try putting a treat on your palm and see if your pet will climb on to your hand. Once it is happy to do this, you can cup your other hand over its back and pick it up.

SAFETY PRECAUTIONS

Hold your hamster over a soft surface when you first pick it up in case it falls. Dwarf hamsters are very difficult to catch if they escape, so it's best to handle them over a box in case they wiggle free.

BE PATIENT

All hamsters are different and it could take up to a month before your pet is ready to be handled. It's important not to force your hamster to do something before it's ready, because stress can cause a serious disease called **wet tail**.

PET TALK

Don't startle me when I'm snoozing. I might think you're a predator and bite you.

MAKING FRIENDS

Once your hamster has settled in, start feeding it a few treats so it can get to know your scent. Be careful! Hamsters have poor eyesight, so if your finger smells like food it might take a bite.

HAMSTER BANQUET

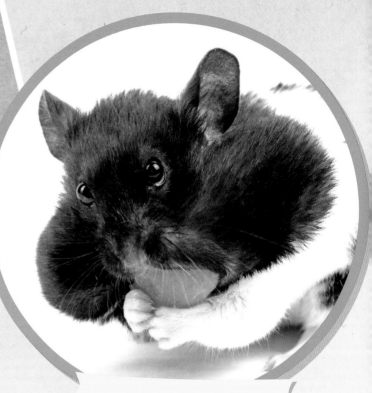

Mixed hamster food provides everything hamsters need, but they also enjoy fruit and vegetables. They eat insects in the wild, so you can give them **mealworms** or tiny pieces of cooked chicken or beef.

The name hamster comes from a German word meaning "to **hoard**."

A HAMSTER'S HOARD

Keeping a well-stocked **larder** is part of a hamster's **instinctive** behavior and allows it to survive in the wild when food is hard to find. Hamsters usually store their favorite foods close to their nest, so they can have a quick snack if they wake up.

PET TALK

Please don't give me sticky food such as peanut butter. It can get stuck in my pouches.

Hamsters like to gnaw on hard dog biscuits because they help to wear down their teeth.

HAMSTERS LOVE:

- Fruit
- Vegetables, including peas, carrots, celery, and broccoli
- Grass and dandelion leaves
- Leafy herbs
- Unsalted peanuts
- Hard-boiled eggs

TINY TREATS

Foods such as fruit, vegetables, or cooked meat should only be given as small treats that your pet can eat right away. If hamsters hoard fresh foods, they may go moldy and spoil the rest of their food store.

DON'T FEED YOUR HAMSTER:

- Apple seeds
- Chocolate
- Citrus fruits
- Garlic or onions
- Kidney beans
- Mushrooms
- Rhubarb
- Almonds

DAY-TO-DAY CARE

Try to spend time with your furry friend every day or it may not stay tame. Play with your hamster in the evening, when it is naturally active.

CAGE CLEANING

Cages need a complete cleaning about once a month. Don't use strongly scented cleaning products, and keep a little of the old bedding and nesting material so the cage smells like home when your hamster goes back in. Save some of the hoarded food and put it back in the same place, or your pet will think that a predator has stolen it.

I use my sense of smell to find my way around my home. That's why I don't like you to wash my scent away when you clean.

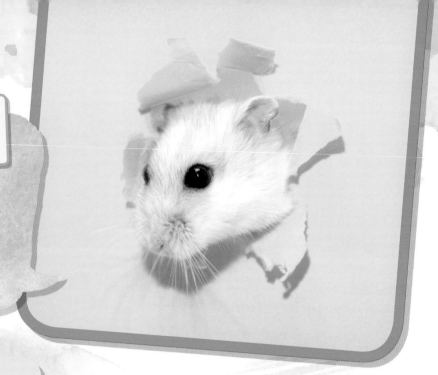

DAILY CHORES

Hamsters don't like having their cages cleaned, so it's best to just remove any dirty bedding and fresh food that might go moldy. If your hamster has a big stash of hoarded food, feed it smaller amounts for a few days. Water should be replaced regularly.

OVERGROWN CLAWS

It's difficult to clip a hamster's claws, so if you notice that your pet's claws are getting too long, try putting some fine sandpaper in a box with some toys and let your hamster run on it for a while. The rough surface should wear its claws down.

This hamster has broken one of its top teeth.

DENTAL CHECK-UP

Hamsters sometimes break a tooth, especially as they get older, so ask an adult to help you check your pet's teeth regularly. A broken tooth can cause the opposite tooth to grow too long, so it might need to be trimmed.

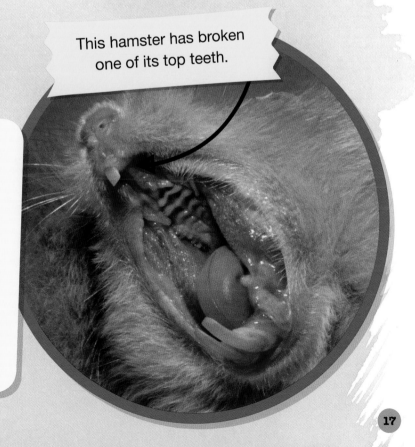

HEALTH AND SAFETY

Small animals can get sick very quickly, so you should check your pet for signs of illness or injury every day. When you get to know your hamster, you will notice any changes in its usual behavior.

WET TAIL

This deadly disease is often caused by stress. Affected hamsters will be weak, have watery diarrhea, and may squeal with pain. If your pet has these symptoms, it needs to go to the vet right away.

Don't allow cats and dogs in the same room as your hamster because it will be frightened by their scent.

DIABETES

Diabetes can affect all hamsters, but it's most often seen in dwarf breeds. Therefore, it's best to keep dwarf hamsters on a low-sugar diet, avoiding fruit and sweet vegetables, such as carrots, corn, and peas. Diabetic hamsters drink much more than usual and may shake or tremble.

PET TALK

I can't see very well and sometimes don't realize how high up I am. I can easily fall and hurt myself.

HEALTH CHECK ☑

Take your hamster to a vet if it:

- stops eating or drinking
- has diarrhea
- suddenly becomes aggressive
- sits in a hunched position
- scratches a lot in one place
- has difficulty walking
- is breathing noisily

COLDS AND FLU

Hamsters can catch colds and flu from humans, so don't handle your pet if you are ill. (Hamsters may infect humans, too.) A hamster should recover in a few days, but if it doesn't, take it to the vet.

HAMSTER BEHAVIOR

In the wild, hamsters sleep in underground burrows during the day and come out at night to search for food. If your hamster's cage is in a brightly lit spot in the evening, it will think it's still daytime and won't get up to play.

KEEP OUT!

Hamsters are especially protective of their nest and food store. If you put your hand into their bed, or change the nesting material too often, your pet will feel that its home is being invaded and it may not feel safe there.

HANDS OFF!

Don't remove a hamster's food hoard unless it's going moldy. Hamsters usually sort through their larder themselves and throw out any food that's no good. If hamsters think their food is being stolen, they sometimes spray it with urine to warn **scavengers** to stay away.

HIBERNATION

If a Syrian hamster gets cold, it may go into **hibernation**, so you should keep your pet's cage in a warm place in the winter. A hibernating hamster will look lifeless and some owners have actually buried their hibernating pet by mistake. If you think your hamster may be hibernating, warm it up slowly and give it small sips of water.

KEEPING THE PEACE

When you have more than one dwarf hamster in a cage, they sometimes fight. If this happens, you may need to give each one its own water bottle, wheel, food bowl, bedroom, and toys. Most dwarf hamsters are happy to share, but some males get territorial and bully their cage mates.

TERRITORIAL BEHAVIOR

Hamsters mark their territory using scent **glands**. These are found on the hips of Syrian hamsters, and on the stomach of dwarf breeds. If your pet spends a long time washing and grooming, it is scenting its paws so it can mark any new territory and find its way home.

COMMUNICATION

The sounds hamsters use to talk to one another are so high-pitched that humans can't hear them. If you understand their **body language**, you can work out what your pet is thinking.

BODY TALK

Here's a guide to what your hamster's body positions mean:

- **Ears up:** I'm curious
- **Stretching or yawning:** I'm relaxed
- **Ears forward with cheek pouches puffed up and mouth open:** I'm frightened
- **Lying on back with teeth showing:** I'm frightened—leave me alone!
- **Freezing completely still:** I've heard something unusual
- **Grooming:** I feel happy and safe
- **Ears back with narrowed eyes:** I'm suspicious

BACK OFF!

Occasionally you might hear your hamster squeak, hiss, screech, or grind its teeth, especially when you first bring it home. All these noises mean that your pet is afraid or annoyed, and it wants to be left alone.

Talk gently to your pet so it gets to know your voice. If you give it treats, it will soon recognize you as a friend.

BITING

Unless your hamster has mistaken your finger for food, a bite is a message that your pet is frightened or ill and doesn't want to be picked up. Don't blame your hamster—this is instinctive behavior and it's the only way your pet can defend itself.

PET TALK

I get scared by loud noises, so please try to be quiet near my cage.

23

TRAINING

Hamsters are quite clever and learn quickly, especially if they get a food reward. Once you have a good relationship with your pet, you can train it to come when you call and to perform simple tricks.

HEY, HAMMY!

If you say your hamster's name each time you give it a treat, your pet should soon learn to come to you. This means you won't need to put your hand into its nest area when you want to take it out of the cage.

STANDING TALL

Show your hamster a treat and then hold it above your pet's head. Say "Stand!" as your hamster reaches for the treat. Continue doing this, raising the treat a little higher each time. Soon, when your pet hears the word "Stand!" it will stand on its hind legs and wait for the treat.

Sunflower seeds are one of a hamster's favorite foods. They are just the right size for a treat.

JUMPING THROUGH A HOOP

You can make a hoop from cardboard, or use a large bracelet. Put the hoop on the ground in front of your hamster and hold a treat on the other side. Say the word "Jump" as your hamster goes through the hoop to reach the treat. Try holding the hoop a little higher once your pet has got the idea.

LITTER-TRAINING

Hamsters usually go to the toilet in the same place, so you can make cage cleaning easier by training your pet to use a large glass jar instead. Lie the jar on its side in your pet's chosen spot and put some clean bedding material or litter inside. Add a little soiled bedding to encourage your pet to use the jar.

PET TALK

Please only teach me one trick at a time because I might get confused.

FUN AND GAMES

You should spend at least an hour a day playing with your hamster. Give your furry friend a chance to run around outside its cage, but don't forget that hamsters are expert escape artists and can squeeze through the tiniest gaps.

Wooden toys give your hamster something to gnaw and help to wear down its teeth.

BOREDOM BUSTER

Hamsters are born burrowers, so they will really enjoy digging in a deep box of sand, shredded paper, or compost. Keep the box on an old sheet or a piece of plastic so you can clean up any mess easily.

ON A ROLL

A hamster ball lets your pet explore without the risk of it disappearing through a hole in the floor or chewing something it shouldn't. Never use a ball at the top of a staircase, and don't keep hamsters in a ball for more than about 15 minutes in case they overheat.

PET TALK

I love tunnels and chewing, so an old cardboard tube is the perfect toy for me.

HAMSTER PLAYGROUND

Hamsters, especially speedy dwarf breeds, can be hard to catch, so it's best to let them run around in an enclosed space, such as a large box or a dry bathtub (with the plug firmly in place). Make sure they have plenty of toys, tubes, and hiding spots to keep them entertained.

SET A HAMSTER TRAP

If your hamster escapes, you may be able to capture it using a bucket or wastepaper bin. Put some padding in the bottom so your hamster has a soft landing if it falls in, then add some of your pet's favorite food. Make a little staircase up the outside of the bucket or bin using books or blocks of wood.

HAMSTER QUIZ

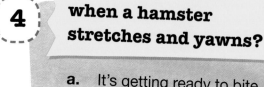

How much do you know about your hamster pal? Take this quiz to find out.

1 **What is unusual about Russian winter white hamsters?**

a. They are all white
b. Their fur gets lighter in winter
c. They hibernate through the winter

2 **Which of these hamster breeds has long hair?**

a. Teddy Bear
b. Chinese
c. Roborovski

3 **Why are Chinese hamsters sometimes called "mousters"?**

a. Because they chase mice
b. Because they squeak a lot
c. Because they look like mice

4 **What does it mean when a hamster stretches and yawns?**

a. It's getting ready to bite
b. It's sleepy
c. It's feeling relaxed

5 **Why shouldn't hamsters have peanut butter?**

a. It upsets their stomachs
b. It's too fattening
c. It gets stuck in their pouches

6 How long do Syrian hamsters live, on average?

a. 18 months
b. Three years
c. Eight years

10 When are hamsters most active?

a. Mid-morning
b. Mid-afternoon
c. In the evening and at night

7 Why do hamsters chew all the time?

a. They are hungry
b. They are bored
c. They need to wear their teeth down

8 Which of these foods is bad for hamsters?

a. Carrot
b. Chocolate
c. Chicken

9 How many Syrian hamsters can live together in one cage?

a. One
b. A pair
c. Three or more

QUIZ ANSWERS

1 What is unusual about Russian winter white hamsters?

c. Their fur gets lighter in the winter

2 Which of these hamster breeds has long hair?

a. Teddy Bear

3 Why are Chinese hamsters sometimes called "mousters"?

c. Because they look like mice

4 What does it mean when a hamster stretches and yawns?

c. It's feeling relaxed

5 Why shouldn't hamsters have peanut butter?

c. It gets stuck in their pouches

6 How long do Syrian hamsters live, on average?

b. Three years

7 Why do hamsters chew all the time?

c. They need to wear their teeth down

8 Which of these foods is bad for hamsters?

b. Chocolate

9 How many Syrian hamsters can live together in one cage?

a. One

10 When are hamsters most active?

c. In the evening and at night

LEARNING MORE

BOOKS

Ganeri, Anita. *Nibble's Guide to Caring for Your Hamster*. Heinemann-Raintree, 2013.

Oliver, Carin. *Homemade for Hamsters*. Firefly Books, 2016.

Sjonger, Rebecca, and Bobbie Kalman. *Hamsters*. Crabtree Publishing Company, 2004.

WEBSITES

www.lovethatpet.com/small-pets/hamsters/
This website is full of helpful information about hamster care.

http://pbskids.org/itsmylife/family/pets/article7.html
Check out this site for fun pet facts and great tips on caring for your hamster.

www.humanesociety.org/animals/hamsters/?credit=web_id139895298
Visit this site for all kinds of tips on how to be the perfect pal to your hamster.

GLOSSARY

body language Communicating through gestures and body movement

breed A group of animals with the same ancestors and characteristics

burrow A hole or tunnel dug by a small animal

color-blind Not able to see the difference between certain colors

diabetes A disease which stops the body from absorbing sugar properly

glands Organs that make fluids and chemicals, such as saliva, tears, and scent

hibernation To be in a deep sleep

hoard A hidden supply that is stored for future use

instinctive Natural behavior that is automatic and not learned

larder A place where food is stored

mealworms Beetle grubs that are dried and sold as food for small animals

predator An animal that hunts and eats other animals

ruff A frill of longer fur around the neck

scavenger An animal that takes discarded or unattended food from other animals

tame To make an animal gentle and obedient

territorial When an animal claims an area for itself and defends it against intruders

ultrasonic A very high sound that humans cannot hear

wet tail A dangerous disease that can develop in a hamster's intestines

INDEX